CHOSEN
to Believe

CHOSEN
to Believe

ROBERTA PETTIT

Published in Houston, Texas, by Writer Launch
First Edition

ISBN: 978-1-948252-04-1

RELIGION / Christian Life / Personal Growth

Writer Launch provides assistance to first-time and veteran authors as they navigate the ins and outs of self-publishing. A division of boutique publisher Battle Ground Creative, Writer Launch is based in Space City—Houston, Texas. To learn more about how we partner with authors, please visit www.writerlaunch.today. *Today is the day to leave your mark!*

Unless otherwise noted, Scripture quotations are taken from THE HOLY BIBLE, NEW INTERNATIONAL VERSION®, NIV® Copyright © 1973, 1978, 1984, 2011 by Biblica, Inc.® Used by permission. All rights reserved worldwide.

Scripture quotations marked "NKJV" are taken from the New King James Version®. Copyright © 1982 by Thomas Nelson. Used by permission. All rights reserved.

Editor: Jared Stump
Cover design: Corinne Karl
Interior design and typeset: Katherine Lloyd, The DESK

Printed in the United States of America

CONTENTS

A BRIEF HISTORY OF THE JEWISH FAITH 7

A CHOSEN PEOPLE 15

WHY I BELIEVE 29

ENDNOTES 43

A BRIEF HISTORY
OF THE JEWISH FAITH

We, as Jews, often have a limited understanding of our Judaism. We understand that we are Jews, that we believe in one God (although the definition of what that means to each individual may vary) and that the Old Testament is our Bible. Much of what we know and practice about our faith is defined by Hebrew school, major holidays, life-cycle events, and keeping the Sabbath. Yet, we often do not have an understanding or knowledge about what the Bible actually teaches and how that played out in early history, much less how these teachings apply to our lives today.

In his book, *A Short History of the Jewish People*, Raymond Scheindlin puts it this way: "… the Jewish people and the Jewish religion are not at all the same thing, certainly not in modern times. On the threshold of the twenty-first century, relatively few Jews in the world are defined as Jews primarily by religious belief or behavior, and the vast majority of Jews in the world—even many of those who are actively Jewish—would be hard-pressed to give a coherent account of Jewish religious doctrine and practice. Although most Jews would probably not put it this way, it is reasonable to maintain that the Jews are a people who share not a religion, but a history."[1]

It's not surprising that we, as a Jewish people, have lost a basic understanding of the Scriptures. As one author stated, "Were a Jew of the generation of Moses or Solomon or Judah the Maccabee alive today, he would be quite confused as he observed our religious conduct."[2]

How did this happen? How did we get here?

To begin with, during Biblical times, the Temple was the central place of worship. The major Jewish festivals, such as Passover or Shavuot, took place at the Temple.

There was an order of priests, the religious leaders of the time, who performed the daily sacrifices as prescribed in the Torah itself. All of this was to be done at the Temple. However, after the Temple was destroyed in 70 CE[3], the Jewish people were unable to fulfill the law as it was written and understood, particularly in relation to sacrifices. Therefore, Judaism changed and began the process of coming to be what we know it as today.

We will explore this system of sacrifices and Temple worship in more depth later, but for now what is important to understand is there was a shift in Jewish practice. "In the period after the destruction of the Temple in Jerusalem, talmud Torah (along with liturgical prayer) replaced sacrifices as the primary means of worship."[4] As the shift in leadership went from the priests to the rabbis, known to be scholars of the Law, "The rabbis even declared talmud Torah to be greater than the daily sacrificial offering and greater even then building the Temple. Rather than a less desirable replacement for a lost system, the talmud Torah becomes a preferred means of divine worship."[5]

With the center of Jewish life destroyed, how was

Judaism to continue? Where were the holidays to be celebrated and how could sacrifices be made? This was the beginning of Rabbinic Judaism.

The rabbis, teachers who were non-priestly specialists, began to take charge of the reorganization of religious life. The emphasis and focus of Judaism became the study of written Torah, along with the oral traditions that had become associated with the Torah. During this time the synagogue emerged as a central institution for religious life. It was here that Jews met for prayer and Torah study. Synagogues became plentiful, allowing Judaism to continue without the Temple. In addition, because sacrifices to atone for sin could no longer be offered at the Temple, the rabbis stressed atonement through good deeds, prayer, and the study of Torah. Even from this brief discussion it is apparent that for a Jew from biblical times to "understand contemporary Jewish observance … he would have to learn that the laws of the Bible, although primary and central, are not the only source of Jewish practice."[6]

The shift to Rabbinic Judaism began with oral teachings believed to have been passed down from the time of Moses. In Rabbinic Judaism, it is believed that Moses received the law and all its explanation on Mount Sinai with the Ten Commandments. It is understood that the Ten Commandments and many of these laws were written down over time in what is now known as the Torah, but there were many more instructions from God to Moses that were transmitted only by word of mouth.

From this time, through the years that followed the destruction of the Temple in 70 CE, the Rabbis met to discuss and understand all that was written in the Torah and all that was handed down from previous generations. At first, the Rabbis did not write down their teachings, but rather passed them on orally from generation to generation. Starting in about 200 CE, Rabbi Yehuda (Judah haNasi) committed these oral teachings to writing in what is called the *Mishnah*. As time passed, the Rabbis interpreted and commented on the Mishnah. Their studies led to what is known as the *Gemara*, where these comments were recorded. Together, the Mishnah and the Gemara are known as the *Talmud*.

Because the study of the Mishnah occurred in two different places, there are two different forms of the Talmud. The Babylonian Talmud was compiled around 500 CE in Babylonia (which is now a part of modern day Iraq) and the Palestinian Talmud which was compiled in the land of Israel around 400 CE. In addition to the Talmud, there is one additional component of Rabbinic Judaism, which is known as the *Midrash*. This often tried to "... fill in the gaps that seem to exist in the text of the Tanach ... through the telling of wonderfully imaginative and interesting stories. Unlike the Mishnah and the Talmud, there is no one single book or set of books called the Midrash."[7] Many of the Midrash were collected and written down between 100 and 1200 CE, but the development of the Midrashim still continues today.

This is Rabbinical Judaism. As you can see, it incorporates much more than the Torah or even the Tanach. The question may arise: Does the Talmud accurately reflect the teachings given in the Tanach? Much study would be required to answer this question in detail, which is beyond the scope and focus of this booklet. Instead, I will focus on the biblical view of what it means to be chosen by God and why I chose to believe that Jesus is the Messiah for all, both Jews and Gentiles alike.

A CHOSEN PEOPLE

od's chosen people. This phrase has been something the Jewish people have come to live by and even die by at times. Being chosen by God is not, after all, something to be taken lightly, but rather a gift to us, really, a gift to treasure and to hold onto. It is the Living God, the Creator of the entire universe who chose us to be called His own.

"For you are a people holy to the LORD your God. The LORD your God has chosen you out of all the peoples on the face of the earth to be His people, His treasured possession" (Deuteronomy 7:6).

God said to the Levites, "… I am giving you the service of the priesthood as a gift …" (Numbers 18:7). If even the service God called us to is a gift, how much more of a gift is it to be chosen as His people, His treasured possession?

But did God intend for the Jewish people alone to be His chosen people, or did He have a much greater purpose in mind? Genesis 1 tells us that God created the earth in its entirety, including those who live on it.

> "And God said, 'Let us make man in our image, after our likeness. They shall rule the fish of the sea, the birds of the sky, the cattle, the whole earth, and all the creeping things that creep on earth.' And God created man in His image, in the image of God, He created him; male and female He created them" (Genesis 1:26-27).[8]

In the beginning there was no distinction, no separation between people. God had not yet called out the Jewish people, but rather created all men and women to be His. Even at the point of Noah and the great flood, when most of mankind had turned away from God, there was not a distinction between Jews and other people. It was not until Abraham (Abram) that God called out a people to be a nation unto Himself.

> "The Lord said to Abram, 'Go forth from your native land and from your father's house to the land that I will show you. I will make you a great nation, and I will bless you. I will make your name great, and you shall be a blessing ...' Abram went forth, as the Lord had commanded him ..." (Genesis 12:1-2, 4).[9]

As we take a closer look at the life of Abraham you may be saying to yourself, "Hold on—who says the Bible is even true, or that Abraham was a real person? And how do I know these 'stories' written in the Torah are true?"

I admit, these questions can be a dividing point for many people. Cunningham and Katzew put it this way, "Two Jews may not believe in the same type of God. One may believe that God wrote the Torah, making it a perfect document. Another may believe that God inspired human beings to write the Torah, making it a holy document. Another may believe that human beings wrote the Torah, making it a historical document."[10] There are still others that question even the historicity of the Torah, discounting the accuracy of what is written therein.

When looking at the life of Abraham and his call by God in the book of Genesis, *The Torah: A Modern Commentary*, describes a shift in the writing, stating, "The book of Genesis, now enters a new phase by moving from myth toward history."[11]

Wow—the Bible as history! Even in this modern commentary of the Torah, the Bible is recognized as a source of historical information. The commentary goes on to say, "He (Abraham) appears as an identifiable person at a certain time. We reach this conclusion because of the nature of his biography and because many details and references are corroborated by sources …"[12]

Although history is important, there is something far deeper in the Bible, something that points to a living God, a God who created us and desires for us to have a relationship with Him. Continuing in the *Modern*

Commentary, we read, "While the authors of the Bible were concerned with history as the recounting of facts, it was the meaning of history that was their primary focus, the account of a spiritual message born of the continuing encounter between God and Abraham's descendants."[13]

Thus, let us return to the story of Abraham and read with both an eye for history and a heart for meaning.

In Genesis 12, Abraham (who was still called Abram at this point in the story) was called, or should we say *chosen*, by God to leave everything he knew and was familiar with to go to a foreign land. God promised Abraham that he will be blessed and made into a great nation, but Abraham had no physical proof that this would happen at the time of his departure. He only believed that he heard the voice of God, and he had the faith necessary to go forth based on what he heard.

God continued to speak to Abraham: "… and all the families of the earth shall bless themselves by you" (Genesis 12:3). Since God created all mankind, could His intention here be for the Jewish nation to lead mankind back to their Creator?

Selah.

What does it really mean to be "chosen" by God? What is God saying to us in the story of Abraham? Is there a purpose that God has for us, even beyond what we may have thought or imagined?

> "You are my witnesses, 'declares the Lord,' and My servant whom I have chosen, in order that you may know and believe Me, and understand that I am He. Before Me there was no god formed, and there will be none after Me. I, even I am the Lord; and there is no Savior *(Deliverer)* besides Me" (Isaiah 43:10-11, italics mine).

Chosen to be witnesses, the Bible tells us. Witnesses of what? Is it possible that we are to be witnesses to the world, to show the world the only true and living God? Some people hate us for the mere fact that we are called *chosen*, seeing us as a people who think we are better than others.

"In the ancient world, every nation but the Jews worshipped its own gods and acknowledged the legitimacy of others' gods. The Jews declared that the gods of the non-Jews were nonsense: 'They have mouths but cannot speak, eyes but cannot see, ears but cannot hear …' (Psalm 115:5-6). There is but one God and He has revealed Himself through the Jews."[14]

"Jewish chosenness has always meant that Jews have believed themselves chosen by God to spread ethical monotheism to the world and to live as a moral 'light unto the nations' (Isaiah 49:6) … The Jews are chosen only to complete a task. This people either chose itself, or as the believing Jew holds, were chosen by God, to make humanity aware of the Supreme Moral Being."[15]

It seems that people who have hated the Jews throughout history have viewed our *chosenness* as a sort of rejection. Yet, as we can see from both the Bible and the writer above, being chosen brought with it a responsibility for the non-Jew [to the nations], to bring the truth of God and His requirements, and, ultimately, His blessings to all people. I wonder if we, as Jews, are doing this today?

It's kind of like the story of Joseph and his dream, which is found in the book of Genesis. Chapter 37 describes him as a young man, only seventeen years of age. He was greatly loved by his father, Jacob, which in turn made his older brothers very angry. Jacob even went so far as to make him a "richly ornamental robe," known to many today as Joseph's "coat of many colors." Joseph then had two dreams in which he was portrayed to reign over his brothers. Like many seventeen-year-olds would, he shared these dreams with his brothers and actually told them they would end up bowing down to him. If they already had a reason to be jealous and angry with Joseph, this gave them even more reason to reject him. Joseph's dreams put him in a position above his brothers (in the sense of a higher rank), as if he had been chosen over his brothers. They hated him for this, and plotted to kill him. However, one of Joseph's brothers was sympathetic and convinced the others to settle for selling him into slavery.

They kept his coat and lied to their father, convincing Jacob that his beloved son Joseph had been killed by wild animals. The story continues in Genesis by chronicling Joseph's life as a slave in Egypt. He quickly found favor with Potiphar, one of Pharaoh's officials, and prospered in Egypt—even as a slave. Yet, even in his prosperity, he found himself set up by Potiphar's wife and when he rejected her advances and refused to sleep with her, she had him put in prison. There also he found favor, and was eventually released by Pharaoh himself. Once again, Joseph was given a place of authority and influence. He used his gift of interpreting dreams to predict that a famine was coming to Egypt and was placed in charge of planning for the impending famine.

Eventually, Joseph's brothers came to Egypt in search of food, as the famine had affected them as well. After an emotional reunion with their brother, they relocate to Egypt and are able to prosper at a time when the famine would have taken their lives. This is definitely the short version of the story, but I think you will be able to see the analogy here. In essence, Joseph was chosen by God to lead the way and provide an avenue of salvation to the Jewish people that would not have been available otherwise. All of Israel survived because of this call on Joseph's life.

So, how does this story relate to the Jewish people and what it means to be "chosen?" As we look at Joseph's life we can see that being "chosen" came with both a cost and a responsibility. We can also see that the purpose of his being chosen was not so much to benefit him personally as it was to benefit the Jewish nation as a whole. I believe it is the same for the Jewish nation today, in that being "chosen" as a Jew is not as much for the Jew himself as it is for all of mankind.

Throughout history the idea of a "chosen people" has created anger and jealousy in people, often leading to severe anti-Semitism, just as Joseph's identification of his calling led to anger and jealousy. This is really just a misunderstanding. Joseph was not called because he was better than his brothers; he was called to save their lives and that of the nation of Israel. In the same way, the Jewish people are not chosen because they are better than other people. If you remember, God created all people. Rather, they were chosen to provide the truth of God and His law to all people and to bring revelation of the one true God, who created every one of us.

Are we reflecting the truth of who God is today?

Let us back up a moment and remember the story of Abraham. He was promised by God that not only would he be made into a great nation—too numerous to count—but that *all* nations would be blessed through him. Is this not the essence of what it means to be chosen? Let's look for a moment at what the Bible tells us about being chosen.

> "Abraham will surely become a great and powerful nation, and all nations on earth will be blessed through him. For I have chosen him, so that he will direct his children and his household after him to keep the way of the LORD by doing what is right and just, so that the LORD will bring about for Abraham what He has promised him" (Genesis 18:18-19).

In this text, being chosen means keeping the way of the Lord and doing what is right and just, according to what God teaches us through His Torah.

> "It is not because you are the most numerous of peoples that the Lord set His heart on you and chose you—indeed; you are the smallest

25

of peoples; but it was because the Lord loved you and kept the oath He made to your fathers that the Lord freed you with a mighty hand ..." (Deuteronomy 7:7-8).[16]

God did not choose the Jewish people because they were better than other people, but because He loved them as He loves all of His creation.

"But now I have chosen Jerusalem for My Name to be there ..." (2 Chronicles 6:6).

Are we carrying and displaying the Name of God? This is the heart of what it means to be chosen.

In conclusion, we as Jews are indeed God's chosen people—chosen by God to carry His Name, and to display His Glory to the world that He Himself created. God chose us because He loved us, not because we did anything wonderful or because we were particularly special. This is our gift, our treasure, and we live to display God's Kingdom reality to the world.

We still live in a land where idols are worshipped and God is forgotten. Our idols now may not be made of stone; perhaps instead they are made of flesh and blood, are found in our many physical treasures, our money, or our possessions. Our idols can even be found running on football fields.

God still desires to reach the nations that He created. It's time for the Jewish people to return to the knowledge of God, to study what is written in the Tanach (the Bible) and to live it out for the sight of the world. As I was reading about Rabbinic Judaism, I came across this statement describing the relationship of the Rabbis: "… Jewish teaching is based on the very special relationship that exists between a teacher and a student."[17] I would challenge you to develop the same type of relationship with the Living God, the creator of the universe, for He is our ultimate teacher.

WHY
I BELIEVE

hy believe in Jesus? Many have asked me why I, after having been raised in a Jewish household where I was clearly taught that Jesus and the New Testament are not a part of the Jewish faith, would I choose to embrace Jesus as my Lord, Savior, and God? I have often pondered this question, yet I have never attempted to articulate the answer in a way that I hope others might understand.

Let me sum up the way in which I came to believe by sharing a statement that Paul made in the book of Galatians, "But I make known to you, brethren, that the gospel which was preached by me is not according to man. For I neither received it from man, nor was taught it, but it came through the revelation of Jesus Christ" (Galatians 1:11-12, NKJV).

So, who was Paul in the New Testament and how did he go from a place of persecuting the Jews who had come to believe in Jesus to becoming a believer himself?

Today, we know him as Paul, but as we look at his background as described in the New Testament we find that his name was actually Saul, often referred to as Saul of Tarsus. In the book of Acts, he writes, "… I am a Jew, from Tarsus in Cilicia, a citizen of no ordinary city…" (Acts 21:39), and again in Acts 22 he says, "I am a Jew, born in Tarsus of Cilicia, but brought up in this city. I studied under Gamaliel and was thoroughly trained in the law of our ancestors. I was just as zealous for God as any of you are today" (Acts 22:3).

Paul tells us several things about who he is in these statements. First, he clarifies that he is a Roman citizen because of his place of birth. From there, he goes on to clearly identify himself as a Jew, thoroughly trained under the teaching of a prominent Rabbi. He also tells us that he lived "zealously" for God. In fact, he was so zealous that he was persecuting the Jews who had chosen to follow Jesus.

> "I (Paul) persecuted the followers of this Way to their death, arresting both men and women and throwing them into prison, as the high priest and all the Council can themselves testify. I even obtained letters from them to their associates in Damascus, and went there to bring these people as prisoners to Jerusalem to be punished" (Acts 22:4-5).

So how did "Saul," the zealous Jew, go from a man trying to destroy those embracing Jesus as their Messiah to believing Jesus was truly the Jewish Messiah? This is the place where Paul's statement in Galatians rings true: "For I neither received it from man, nor was taught it, but it came through the revelation of Jesus Christ" (Galatians 1:12, NKJV).

Paul's experience is retold in Acts 9. As he was traveling to Damascus, letters in hand to take those professing faith in Jesus as prisoners, a "light from heaven flashed around him" (v. 3b). The Scriptures go on to say that "he fell to the ground and heard a voice say to him, 'Saul, Saul, why do you persecute me?' 'Who are you Lord?' Saul asked. 'I am Jesus, whom you are persecuting,' he replied" (v. 4-5).

Now *this* is revelation! Paul wasn't looking or searching for the truth, and he actually already believed he *was* moving in the truth as he worked to stop those who believed in Jesus. He believed he was trying to stop a movement that was working against the Judaism he held close to his heart, when God suddenly revealed Himself. Paul heard the voice of God and could no longer deny that Jesus was the Messiah. Everyone with Paul heard the sound, but did not see or hear what Paul heard.

God went on to seal the work He was doing in Paul, directing him to go to the city of Damascus and wait for further direction. Following this experience, Paul lost his sense of sight for three days and had to be escorted into the city. During those three days, Paul neither ate nor drank, but waited to hear more from God. At the same time, God spoke to another man, Ananias, directing him to go and pray for Paul.

Ananias obeyed God, and after he prayed for Paul his vision was restored. Paul was then baptized, and began to eat again and regain his strength (Acts 9:17-19). Paul was changed following this experience with God, not because he was looking for an experience or spent time researching the truth, but because the God who is alive today showed up in a tangible and powerful way. There was no denying the truth, and Paul went on to share his experience and live the rest of his life for Jesus.

Okay, so what about me? No, I wasn't persecuting believers or even working against those who believed in Jesus, and I wasn't literally knocked off a horse as hearing the bellowing voice of God. Yet, I in a sense was knocked off my horse. I was neither searching for Jesus nor had any thought that Jesus would be the answer for the Jewish people. In fact, I thought back many years after embracing Jesus as the Messiah and remembered that I had been handed tracts (small booklets telling me to confess my sins and accept Jesus as the sacrifice for those sins). At the time, I just tossed them away, simply because I was Jewish and I believed Jesus was not for the Jewish people. Yet, after spending a summer working on a kibbutz in Israel, I returned home to find a friend had become a believer in Jesus as the Messiah. She was not Jewish; yet, the Holy Spirit began to stir my heart and I began to develop a hunger to know why she believed. She didn't try to persuade me, preach to me, or convert me in any way, but God drew me in, and I was stirred to ask about her newfound faith.

As I go on to share my experience and how Jesus entered my life, let me stop and say that everyone does not come to a place of accepting and believing in Jesus in the same manner. God, the Maker of heaven and earth and the Creator of life, loves each and every person He has made and will reveal Himself in a way that is personal for each individual. Look at the lives of the first believers when Jesus made Himself known on earth. You may or may not be aware that all of those who first embraced Jesus were Jewish. Paul, also being Jewish, came to believe following Jesus' death and subsequent resurrection. The first believers, known as disciples, came to believe as they walked with Jesus on the earth and had their faith further solidified after His death and resurrection. Some followed Jesus as they came into contact with Him and witnessed

His healing firsthand. Others, such as Simon Peter, Andrew, James, and John, were specifically called out as they were busy living their lives and working as fishermen.

> "As Jesus was walking beside the Sea of Galilee, he saw two brothers, Simon called Peter and his brother Andrew. They were casting a net into the lake, for they were fishermen. 'Come, follow me,' Jesus said, 'and I will send you out to fish for people. At once they left their nets and followed him. Going on from there, he saw two other brothers, James son of Zebedee and his brother John. They were in a boat with their father Zebedee, preparing their nets. Jesus called them, and immediately they left the boat and their father and followed him" (Matthew 4:18-22).

Even the unlikely responded to Jesus when He called. In Luke 5:27-28, Jesus came across a tax collector by the name of Levi, sitting at his booth. Jesus simply said the words, "Follow me," and Levi got up from his booth, left everything behind, and followed Jesus.

In each of these examples, Jesus showed up, invited people to follow Him, and they did. To pick up and leave home, work, and family, there must have been something in the command of Jesus' voice that drew each of them. My thoughts go to the voice of God. In the Old Testament, the voice of God is described as extremely powerful.

> "The voice of the Lord is over the waters; the God of glory thunders, the Lord thunders over the mighty waters. The voice of the Lord is powerful; the voice of the Lord is majestic. The voice of the Lord breaks the cedars; the Lord breaks in pieces the cedars of Lebanon. … The voice of the Lord strikes with flashes of lightning" (Psalm 29:3-5, 7).

Amos 1:2 tells us that "the Lord roars from Zion," and the Lord responds to Job asking, "Can you thunder with a voice like God's?" (see Job 40:9). In Ezekiel 43:2, the Lord's voice is described as a "roar," and in Exodus 19:19, God answered Moses in thunder.

As we can see from these Scriptures, God's voice comes with power; yet, even when God's voice is not loud like thunder it remains captivating. In 1 Kings 19:12-13, "After the earthquake came a fire, but the LORD was not in the fire. And after the fire came a gentle whisper. When Elijah heard it, he pulled his cloak over his face and went out and stood at the mouth of the cave. Then a voice said to him, 'What are you doing here, Elijah?'"

Elijah heard God's voice as only a whisper, yet with the same impact as others heard God's voice with thunder. Elijah is just one example of the many people who heard God's voice. Moses, Jacob, Abraham, and Job are among others who heard and responded to the voice of God.

So, what brought me to Jesus, to believe that He is the Savior for all people, including the Jewish nation? How did the voice of God impact my understanding and faith? After learning that my friend had been changed by a new relationship with Jesus, I accompanied her to a small gathering where the Bible was read and the message of Jesus as the Messiah and Savior of the world was given. Although there was something that stirred my heart and was drawing me in, I did not choose to believe in Jesus that night. I stood on the side of caution, as I did believe in God as a Jew, yet had great concerns about the possibility of turning my back on God by accepting Jesus. Although Jesus was shared as part of the Trinity of God, it didn't compute with what I was taught or believed. I also grew up with a warning that Christians were out to convert the Jewish nation, ultimately wiping us out. I knew well of the atrocities suffered during the holocaust and some of the history of the persecution to Jews in the name of Jesus, and I was not about to just blindly say "yes" to something I had been taught was so wrong. Yet, I did say yes soon after.

Why did I do this? What caused me to change my mind?

As I returned home that night, my mind was racing as I tried to put together all that was shared that night. My heart continued to race, all the while feeling something very new, something very powerful and very different. I lay in bed that night and began to pray. Prayer was not a foreign concept to me. I believed in God and prayed often, though most of the time it was either a prayer asking forgiveness or a desperate prayer to get me out of some mess I had willingly gotten myself into. This time was different, as I wasn't asking forgiveness or praying in fearful desperation, but was sincerely asking God, "What about Jesus?"

I wanted to know from God if the words shared that night were true. Did Jesus come first for the Jewish nation, as it says in the New Testament?

"I am not ashamed of the gospel, because it is the power of God for the salvation of everyone who believes: first for the Jew, then for the Gentile" (Romans 1:16).

As I asked that very question, I heard the answer. Yes, I heard the voice of God. Did it bellow with thunder or would I even venture to say it was an audible voice? No, but it was still very clear to me. It was much like Elijah heard; a voice not in the earthquake or the fire, but in a gentle whisper. (1 Kings 19:12-13) There was no doubting in that moment. It wasn't the answer I was looking for, but it was clear that the answer was "yes." Yes, Jesus is the

Messiah for the Jewish nation. The struggle ended at that moment, as I gave my life to Jesus that very week.

Jesus has not let me down. Over time, there have been struggles, both with my faith and the everyday battles that are inherent in life itself. Working out the faith came by "revelation," with the knowledge of what I had been taught at times creating conflict, but as I studied the Bible and spent time in prayer, the truth of Jesus ultimately became more apparent. Immediately after saying yes to Jesus, the Bible came alive to me, and over the next couple of years I grew in my understanding of God. There did come a time when I began to question my faith more intensely, but the questions only led me to Jesus once again. There was no denying the truth.

My belief *in* God has been transformed into a relationship *with* God. My Judaism, rather than being lost, has come *alive*. Judaism is truly the foundation of Christianity. As it says in John 4:22, "… Salvation is from the Jews."

It is the Old Testament that prophesied about the coming Messiah and identified Jesus as that Messiah. It is the laws set up from the days of Moses that laid the foundation for repentance through a blood sacrifice. And it is Jesus who provided the final sacrifice, allowing us to enter into a relationship with God today.

"You will seek me and find me when you seek me with all your heart" (Jeremiah 29:13).

"But if from there you seek the LORD your God, you will find him if you seek him with all your heart and with all your soul" (Deuteronomy 4:29).

I would challenge you to seek God, to ask Him, as I did, if He truly is the Jewish Messiah, the savior for the Jewish people. Once you have done this, simply wait. God will answer if you ask Him with a heart that desires to know the truth. The answer may not be instantaneous, but it will come.

As I conclude, the Shema comes to mind: "Hear, O Israel: The LORD our God, the LORD is one" (Deuteronomy 6:4).

Just after the Shema, you will find the beginning words of the prayer we know as the V'ahavta. It goes like this: "Love the LORD your God with all your heart and with all your soul and with all your strength" (Deuteronomy 6:5).

God is one. It is not about Christianity vs. Judaism. They are one, serving the same God who calls us to love Him with all of our hearts and with everything we have. To love God, we will need to seek Him and get to know who He is. It is in this place we will also find Jesus, the Messiah and Savior of the world.

ENDNOTES

1. Raymond P. Scheindlin, *A Short History of the Jewish People: From Legendary Times to Modern Statehood* (Oxford, England: Oxford University Press, 1998), xii.
2. Alfred J. Kolatch, *The Jewish Book of Why* (Middle Village, NY: Jonathan David Publishers, 1981; 1995), 2.
3. CE stands for *common era*. The term AD is also commonly used, which stands for *anno domini—the year of our Lord* in Latin. Because this refers to the birth of Christ, Jewish history more commonly uses CE to designate this calendar shift.
4. My Jewish Learning, "Torah Study: Themes and Theology," *MyJewishLearning.com*, accessed August 2018, http://www.myjewishlearning.com/article/torah-study-themes-and-theology/
5. ibid.
6. Alfred J. Kolatch, *The Jewish Book of Why*, 3.

7. Ellen Singer & Bernard M. Zlotowitz, *Our Sacred Texts* (New York: UAHC Press, 1992), 89.

8. Scripture is taken from the English translation of the Torah, copyright © 1962, 1967 by the Jewish Publication Society.

9. ibid.

10. David Fox Sandmel, Rosann M. Catalano, Christopher M. Leighton, *Irreconcilable Differences? A Learning Resource for Jews and Christians* (Boulder, CO: Westview Press, 2001), 33.

11. W. Gunter Plaut, *The Torah: A Modern Commentary* (New York: Union of American Hebrew Congregations, 1981), 88.

12. ibid.

13. ibid, 89.

14. Dennis Prager & Joseph Telushkin, Why the Jews? (New York: Simon and Schuster, 1983), 28.

15. ibid, 43.

16. Scripture is taken from the English translation of the Torah, copyright © 1962, 1967 by the Jewish Publication Society.

17. Ellen Singer & Bernard M. Zlotowitz, *Our Sacred Texts*, 86.

Made in the USA
Middletown, DE
04 July 2021

43587011R00029